YOU KNOW YOU'RE A CHILD OF THE 2000S WHEN...

CHARLIE ELLIS

summersdale

YOU KNOW YOU'RE A CHILD OF THE 2000s WHEN…

Text by Abi McMahon and Hannah Adams

Illustrations by Rita Kovács; icons © Shutterstock.com
Central Perk vector © Vera Martovskaya/Shutterstock.com

An Hachette UK Company
www.hachette.co.uk

Summersdale Publishers Ltd
Part of Octopus Publishing Group Limited
Carmelite House
50 Victoria Embankment
LONDON
EC4Y 0DZ
UK

www.summersdale.com

Printed and bound in China

ISBN: 978-1-78783-313-5

Substantial discounts on bulk quantities of Summersdale books are available to corporations, professional associations and other organizations. For details contact general enquiries: telephone: +44 (0) 1243 771107, fax: +44 (0) 1243 786300 or email: enquiries@summersdale.com.

To...

From...

DO YOU REMEMBER...

Bratz dolls
···

Oh. Em. Gee. Barbie suddenly looked ancient next to these bobble-headed fashionistas. Dad might not have approved of all the make-up they were wearing, but we knew they were the *coolest*.

Heelys
···

We always knew that walking was for losers and Heelys just proved it! So we knocked down a few people on the way—we still got there faster!

BEYBLADES

At the time we thought these toys were the flashiest, most cutting-edge toys on the market. Looking back, it was basically a spinning top with a bit of extra plastic tacked on. Oh, well, it was fun trying to fight them.

YOU KNOW YOU'RE A CHILD OF THE 2000s WHEN...

After watching an episode of **Drake and Josh,** you couldn't help repeating everything you said for emphasis. EMPHASIS!

The words **"Sun-in"** and
"frosted tips" bring back
awkward memories of
regrettable hairstyles.

When anyone uses the phrase
"it wasn't me," you break out into
a full **Shaggy** impersonation.

Between Listening to **Avril
Lavigne** and **Good Charlotte**,
you thought you were really punk.

QUIZ

ONLY A CHILD OF THE 2000s WILL KNOW...

1 *Twilight* thrilled both teen and adult hearts in the noughties. When was it first published?

2 Who was the author of *Stormbreaker*, the first of the Alex Rider series?

3 What were the three Deathly Hallows in the final Harry Potter book, *Harry Potter and the Deathly Hallows*?

8

What did the Gruffalo encounter in the deep dark woods?

 The Golden Compass, *The Subtle Knife*, and *The Amber Spyglass* are the names of the books of what trilogy?

 In *How I Live Now*, the main character was known as Daisy, but what was her real name?

 Malorie Blackman wrote what critically acclaimed series of young adult novels?

8 In what year was *The Curious Incident of the Dog in Night-Time* published?

YOU KNOW YOU'RE A CHILD OF THE 2000s WHEN...

You still have copies of your best **MSN conversations** saved somewhere.

The most embarrassing moment of your life was when your crush found out you had made a **Sims family** based on the two of you.

Your adventures with **LimeWire** may have infected the family computer more than once.

You still struggle to believe that anyone could ever have put **heels** on sneakers.

DO YOU REMEMBER...

Buffy the Vampire Slayer

Was there anything more kick-ass than Buffy Summers battling the forces of darkness? There she was, fighting supernatural evil, maintaining a social life, and managing to navigate the definition of an "it's complicated" relationship, while we could barely handle our homework. We laughed, we cried, and we wish the show had never ended.

The Wild Thornberrys

Wussy Darwin, wild Donnie, the legendary Nigel—oh, but we loved the Thornberrys. And we never had a go at talking to animals, à la Eliza, honest!

The Suite Life of Zack and Cody

These loveable scamps had a pretty "suite" deal—a whole hotel to run around in and all kinds of mischief to be making in the process. And will there even be a more iconic bell hop than Esteban Julio Ricardo Montoya de la Rosa Ramírez? We think not.

iCarly

Let's be honest, for the first few episodes we kept mistaking Carly for Megan (RIP, *Drake and Josh*). Then we realized that Carly, Sam, and Freddie were actually a dream team, and definitely didn't spend a lot of time actually trying to find the iCarly web show online … It's real, I tell you!

Kim Possible

Sure, there were spies, Kim kicking butt and all sorts of international shenanigans. But what was *Kim Possible* really all about? Who was the real star of the show? That would be Rufus, the naked mole rat. Our parents were quite surprised by our Christmas list that year!

SpongeBob SquarePants

Bet you got the theme song in your head as soon as you read the title! Whether you loved good old SpongeBob sincerely or ironically, you could be sure you had the backpack, the pencil case, and/or the T-shirt. You'd had the SpongeBob kitchen sink if it was available.

YOU KNOW YOU'RE A CHILD OF THE 2000s WHEN...

The phrase **"Dollz Mania"**
sparks real excitement in you.

You're undecided on the **Hubba Bubba** vs **Bubblicious** decision.

Nothing gets you on the dance floor faster than **Pink**'s "Get This Party Started."

When it was actually cool to "look like a baby" with a **Baby Bottle Pop**.

QUIZ

 Who did Lennox Lewis knock out in 2002 to cement his boxing legacy?

 In what year did the Boston Red Sox win the World Series, breaking the eighty-six-year-long "Curse of the Bambino"?

 What athlete won the 100m butterfly at the 2008 Summer Olympics by one-hundredth of a second, earning his eighth gold medal?

What budding thirteen-year-old pop sensation sang the National Anthem before an NBA game in Philadelphia in April 2002?

 Who was named the boxing fighter of the decade by BWAA, WBC, and WBO?

 What NFL starting quarterback has won more Super Bowls than any other in history?

 Usain Bolt smashed the 100m and 200m world records at which Olympics?

 What years did Roger Federer NOT win the Wimbledon Men's Singles title?

YOU KNOW YOU'RE A CHILD OF THE 2000s WHEN...

You're pretty sure that **crimped hair** will come back into fashion at some point soon.

You still can't believe **Jennifer Hudson** took *seventh place* on American Idol.

You can still remember when **floppy disks**, not USBs, were the removable storage drive of choice.

You or someone you know was way too obsessed with **Sudoku** puzzles.

The Moment of Truth

Maybe the most uncomfortable viewing experience ever, this was a show that made us seriously question if money was really *that* important. If this show was designed to be a train wreck, it succeeded—but man, was it entertaining.

Alias

As a show that reshaped the sci-fi genre, Sydney was a trailblazer for strong female leads. To this day, we can't see a red wig without wanting to put on a pair of black leather trousers and change our identity.

FRIENDS

Rachel, Ross, Monica, Chandler, Joey, and Phoebe stole our hearts for the whole of the noughties, and we're pretty sure they still have them today. We've all lost count of how many times we've watched this, and we have absolutely no shame about it.

YOU KNOW YOU'RE
A CHILD OF THE
2000s
WHEN...

You have your **milkshake**: you're wondering why there are no boys in your yard.

Your first foray into the world of composing was making **monotone ringtones** on your Nokia.

Your drawers are full of **wristbands** in aid of charities.

You have zero regrets about your **fashion poncho** collection.

QUIZ

ONLY A CHILD OF THE 2000s WILL KNOW...

 In her song "Party in the U.S.A.," at what airport did Miley Cyrus hop off the plane?

 After what animal was a famously ugly plastic shoe named?

 What high-energy dance-based form of exercise became popular in the noughties?

 What type of fish was Big Mouth Billy?

5 Kim Kardashian's stepbrother was featured on what reality show?

6 LimeWire was used for what?

7 Goku, Piccolo, and Vegeta are all characters from what series?

8 What was unique about the gel pens everyone went crazy for in the noughties?

YOU KNOW YOU'RE A CHILD OF THE 2000s WHEN...

You practically glued your lips together every time you applied **lip gloss**.

James Blunt's "You're Beautiful" is the most romantic song in the world to you.

The biggest falling out of your teen life was when you discovered you weren't in your bestie's top-eight **Myspace** friends.

You are still washing the **hair mascara** out.

The Dark Knight

Batman Begins happened, of course. And we were sort of excited about *The Dark Knight*, sure. But then we saw it and it blew every superhero film we'd ever seen out the water. Christian Bale's husky Batman voice, Heath Ledger's cray Joker—it had the goods.

Lord of the Rings: The Return of the King

The plot of this film is, as far as we can remember, Legolas surfs an elephant, Gimli can't see, and Sam is a boss from start to finish. That and the hundred different endings. It was magnificent and we probably have it to thank for *Game of Thrones*.

Casino Royale

After the invisible car and Madonna fiasco, it was looking like Bond would never be cool again. When Daniel Craig was cast, we were even more sure of that fact. And yet how wrong we were—gambling, shadowy villains, and heartbreaking women, Bond was back.

American Pie

The noughties were prime time for gross-out comedies full of sex and clueless teen boys. None were quite as gross-out and full of sex as the American Pie series (even if there was a touching romantic storyline with Finch and Stifler's mom).

Finding Nemo

There are two addresses that I can guarantee you have memorized. One will be your own. And the other will be P. Sherman, 42 Wallaby Way, Sydney.

Mean Girls

This. Film. Was. Iconic. It looked like it was going to be just another teen comedy and then turned out to be a quotable, hilarious masterpiece. Hands up if you can perform Kevin G's rap.

YOU KNOW YOU'RE A CHILD OF THE 2000s WHEN...

You spent half your weekly **allowance** on pick "n" mix from Walmart.

You are a card-carrying member of either **Team Edward** or **Team Jacob**.

Your parents didn't let you get a **Mohawk**, so you compromised with a fauxhawk.

There wasn't a hairstyle that wasn't improved by adding a **mini-quiff**.

QUIZ

 What type of M&M's were discontinued in 2005 (only to be brought back by popular demand in 2015)?

 Outrageous Original and Cool Cola are both flavors of what chewing gum?

 In 2006, Nestlé caused a minor panic among children when they did what to Smarties?

 What contentious Tic Tac flavor was discontinued in 2009?

5 What special Doritos range was discontinued in 2005?

6 In what year did Sprinkles, one of the first US cupcake bakeries, open in Beverly Hills?

7 What spherical Nestlé treat was relaunched in the 2000s, this time filled with hard candy instead of their original inedible prizes?

8 What were the three original flavors of Astro Pops?

YOU KNOW YOU'RE
A CHILD OF THE
2000s
WHEN...

You still believe you can **wingardium leviosa** objects toward you when you're feeling lazy.

You were twelve and owned more **pashminas** than your grandma.

You thought your **mismatched earrings** were the height of quirky fashion.

You can only say the word **"donkey"** in a Scottish accent.

Popped collar polos

Looking back, it isn't clear why we thought wearing our collars up around our ears was such a great idea. Perhaps it was to look bigger to predators and rivals. Perhaps we were just really ashamed of our necks. Either way, those collars had to be popped.

Cardigans

In a trend our grandad was happy to see return, menswear was all about the cardigan. No longer was the humble cardigan a sure-fire sign that you were a total nerd; now it was the cool kids who wore them.

HOODIES UNDER BLAZERS

The noughties were all about looks that were formal yet informal. If they could be summed up in a clothing style, then they would be "smart casual." We reached peak smart casual with the ultimate clash of office wear and comfort: the hoodie worn under the blazer.

YOU KNOW YOU'RE
A CHILD OF THE
2000s
WHEN...

Everything you said was
carefully planned to be as
"random" as possible.

Your journey into the world of music started with **My Chemical Romance** and **Good Charlotte**.

You and your friends sustained more than a few **injuries** trying your own *Jackass* stunts.

You diligently practiced your best **bullet-dodging** technique, à la *The Matrix*.

QUIZ

ONLY A CHILD OF THE 2000s WILL KNOW...

 How long was Britney Spears married to her childhood sweetheart for?

 Janet Jackson lost part of her costume during a Super Bowl performance, showing what body part?

3 Who was the highest-paid actress of the noughties?

4 In a 2005 interview with Oprah Winfrey, what did Tom Cruise famously do while expressing his love for new girlfriend Katie Holmes?

In 2009 Kanye West's infamous interruption of Taylor Swift at the MTV Video Music Awards turned into what meme?

 Teen sweethearts Zac Efron and Vanessa Hudgens met on the set of what Disney film?

 In 2001, Winona Ryder was caught committing what illegal act?

 In 2002, who became the first female winner of *Big Brother*?

YOU KNOW YOU'RE A CHILD OF THE 2000s WHEN...

Eyeliner companies hadn't done such a roaring trade since the sixties.

You pulled your hair into such a **tight ponytail**, you looked years younger (practically single figures).

You would use **highlighter** and tippex to give yourself a funky manicure.

You thought **platform flip-flops** were so much more chic than regular, flat flip-flops.

DO YOU REMEMBER...

Skinny jeans

Ah skinny jeans, those glorious leg-numbing fashion items. We all heard the stories about a friend of a friend of a friend who had to be cut out of her jeans by the fire service and rushed to hospital, but it was never enough to deter us from squeezing into our skinnies.

Hippie dresses over flared jeans

One of those "styles" it's better to forget. The jeans were meant to add some "edge" to those floaty, floral dresses, but looking at the photos, they seem to just add "doesn't know how to dress herself" vibes.

Blazers

These were almost always paired with skinnies and the straightest hair ever, creating a look so sleek it must have been aerodynamic.

Denim miniskirts

The beloved denim skirt's hemline rose throughout the noughties until it was essentially just a denim belt—and who can forget Christina Aguilera's iconic 2002 VMA look? Skirt or belt has never been a more pressing question.

Ugg boots

The most expensive pair of outdoor slippers ever to be made, these babies had us begging relatives who were holidaying abroad to chuck all their clothes and just fill their suitcases with Ugg boots to bring back for us. Most commonly seen paired with...

Juicy Couture velour tracksuits

OK, so maybe we didn't look very stylish, but we were definitely comfortable. Still, better not to remember that time we all went around with "juicy" branded across our bums.

YOU KNOW YOU'RE A CHILD OF THE 2000s WHEN...

You spent more on **flavored lip balms** than on candy.

You did virtually no exercise but still always wore **chequered sweatbands**.

You had to throw out all your baseball caps and buy **trucker caps**.

You thought a **tie** and T-shirt was the ultimate in cutting-edge fashion.

QUIZ

ONLY A CHILD OF THE 2000s WILL KNOW...

 In what year did the Apple iPhone first hit stores?

 What all-time bestselling console was released in 2000?

 This iconic noughties video game has become the best-selling game of all time. What was it?

 In what year did the iTunes Music Store launch?

What was Facebook's original name?

 What was Motorola's bestselling flip phone called?

 In 2005, MSN Messenger was rebranded as what?

 In what year did Dyson release its mind-blowing new hand dryer, the Airblade?

Answers: 1. 2007; **2.** PlayStation 2; **3.** Wii Sports; **4.** 2003; **5.** Thefacebook; **6.** Razr; **7.** Windows Live Messenger; **8.** 2006

YOU KNOW YOU'RE A CHILD OF THE 2000s WHEN...

Your mom had to cut you out of your **skinny jeans** at least once.

Your **fringe** was permanently plastered to one side of your face.

You owned a **keffiyeh** scarf in every color.

You know for sure that **Heath Ledger**'s Joker is the best Joker.

Chunky highlights

Bye-bye, subtle dye job, hello wearing your highlights as a badge of pride. The aim wasn't to look natural—the aim was to assert your dominance by having as many different colors, in the widest swathes possible, plastered all over your head.

Spiked hair

While girls were aiming for a "camo" effect with their hair, guys were rocking some electric shock chic with their hair. It could be gelled straight up, it could be gelled to the side, it could be gelled in every direction—but it had to be gelled!

BIEBER HAIR

Whether you were an emo or a Belieber, where your musical tastes differed your hairstyle was the same. The only downside: your grandparents wouldn't stop making lame jokes about you not being able to see with all that hair in your eyes.

YOU KNOW YOU'RE A CHILD OF THE 2000s WHEN...

Your parents have never forgiven you for lying about exactly what happens in a *Grand Theft Auto* game.

Family Guy and **South Park** sessions with your friends were a must.

If you could have an ironic children's **cartoon pencil case** for work, you totes would.

You still use the phrase "**totes**."

QUIZ

ONLY A CHILD OF THE 2000s WILL KNOW...

 1 How many terms did George W. Bush serve as president of the United States for?

 2 In what year was Nancy Pelosi, the first female speaker of the House of Representatives, sworn into office?

 3 How many seasons did *Friends* run for before ending in 2004?

 4 What confident contestant was eliminated from cycle 6 of *America's Next Top Model*, making an infamous exit?

5 What was the name of the device used to record films and TV shows before DVDs?

6 An iconic Budweiser commercial campaign introduced what new pop culture catchphrase to the world?

7 In what year did Pluto get declassified from planet to dwarf planet?

8 Who won the first season of *American Idol* in September 2002?

YOU KNOW YOU'RE A CHILD OF THE 2000s WHEN...

You're still not completely clear on what the **Millennium Bug** entailed.

You and your friends read every **John Green book** (and cried at some point during all of them).

You own an unworn pair of **gold hot pants**, à la Kylie.

You remember when your main concern in each day was keeping your **Tamagotchi** alive.

"Hey Ya!" by OutKast

Outkast are some sort of wizards, because every time we hear this song, we *still* automatically stretch out our arms and wiggle our fingers and then shake it much in the manner of a Polaroid picture. It's like we can't help ourselves.

"Bye Bye Bye" by NSYNC

NSYNC were already on the list of our favorite boy bands, but after this song came out, we somehow grew even more obsessed. We'd never say bye bye bye to you boys—especially not you, Justin.

"The Black Parade" by My Chemical Romance

Take yourself back to the times when you only wanted to wear clothes that were black and decorated with skulls, when you brushed your hair over one eye and declared *this isn't a phase, Mom*. Oh yes, I'm talking about the My Chemical Romance days. I'm sorry to remind you.

"Last Nite" by The Strokes

All it takes is this song to come on at the club and you find yourself with your arms wrapped around strangers, jumping up and down like an utter lunatic.

"Feel Good Inc." by Gorillaz

We didn't know quite what to make of this song when it first came out and yet within a few listens we couldn't get that hook out of our heads.

"I Kissed a Girl" by Katy Perry

It seems a bit tame nowadays, but at the time "I Kissed a Girl" caused quite the scandal! Bless, we were so much more innocent in those days.

YOU KNOW YOU'RE A CHILD OF THE 2000s WHEN...

You saw all of **Adam Sandler's** movies even though your parents didn't approve.

You recall having to type your **emojis** out by hand.

You're fluent in **Baltimore** slang, thanks to *The Wire*.

You sort of still fancy **Freddie Prinze, Jr**.

QUIZ

ONLY A CHILD OF THE 2000s WILL KNOW...

 1 Does the term "meh" indicate you are for, against, or unfussed by something?

2 What does ROFL mean?

 3 What is a bromance?

 4 "Pwned" and "1337" are words from what language?

5 The slang term for an older woman seeking romantic relationships with younger men became popular. What is it?

6 Glamping is an offshoot of what activity?

7 Before *Drake and Josh*, Drake Bell and Josh Peck appeared together on what Nickelodeon show?

Answers: 1. Untussed; **2.** Roll On the Floor Laughing; **3.** A close friendship between two men; **4.** Leetspeak; **5.** Cougar; **6.** Camping; **7.** *The Amanda Show*

65

YOU KNOW YOU'RE
A CHILD OF THE
2000s
WHEN...

You're sort of glad that **documentaries** aren't such a "thing" anymore, no offense, Michael Moore.

You know where you were when **"Crazy in Love"** dropped.

You had your own graffiti **"street name"** for a while and tried to make your mom call you by it.

You haven't worked out whether *The Da Vinci Code* was real or made up.

DO YOU REMEMBER...

MILF

Thank you, *American pie*, for that charming phrase. We lived in fear that someone would refer to our mother using that word—gross.

Chillin'

Was "Wot U up 2?" and "Chillin'" the most texted conversation of the noughties? Possibly. Not up to much? You were chillin'. Out and about? You were chillin'. Doing literally anything at any time? Chillin'.

Fetch

Stop trying to make "fetch" happen, Gretchen.

TEXT SPEAK

How r U? Gr8. LOL. For a moment it
seemed like we had revolutionized
language forever, so how come we're back
to using full words? Oh yes, smartphones.
I suppose that the ability to access music,
films, the Internet,
and a whole
world of apps
makes up for the
loss of utterly
unintelligible
language.

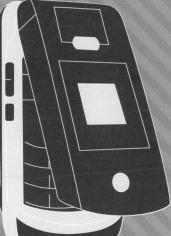

YOU KNOW YOU'RE
A CHILD OF THE
2000s
WHEN...

Your first foray into **naughty internet content** was Belle de Jour's blog.

You have an abandoned **blog** of your own somewhere.

To you, **Tom Welling** will always be Clark Kent.

You sincerely hope that no one ever turns up to **pimp your ride**.

QUIZ

ONLY A CHILD OF
THE 2000s WILL KNOW...

 1 What animal had been let out in the Baha Men's hit single?

 2 "The Rock Show" was a single from which Blink 182 album?

 3 What rapper featured on Beyoncé's single, "Crazy in Love"?

 4 What band, whose breakthrough single was "Harder to Breathe," was originally called Kara's Flowers?

5 Name the two members of Outkast.

6 In what year was The Street's "When You Wasn't Famous" released?

7 What activity was taking place in the video for Eric Prydz's single "Call on Me"?

8 What was the name of Gnarls Barkley's breakthrough single?

YOU KNOW YOU'RE A CHILD OF THE 2000s WHEN...

Your introduction to opera was from *Jerry Springer: The Opera*. Who said you weren't cultured?

You snuck in to the first **Saw** film.

You still think **Buffy** and Angel belong together.

... And it still causes you pain to remember Tara being shot. **Twillow** forever.

Blink 182

For some noughties kids, Blink weren't just a band—they were a lifestyle. Combined with a mostly unused skateboard under one arm, Dickies shorts and long socks and a healthy diet of *Jackass*, Blink 182 were all you needed.

Eminem

May I have your attention, please? This controversial hip-hop icon came to define 2000s music. Whether you liked him or not, you couldn't throw shade over his ability to spit rhymes at lightning speed.

Arctic Monkeys

Among all the military jackets and shoe-gazing poetry of the Indie movement came one thunderous, game-changing single. "I Bet You Look Good on the Dancefloor" blew everyone away, and Arctic Monkeys have been great ever since.

Amy Winehouse

Oh, Amy. With her big beehive and bigger voice, she blew our minds with her retro-modern sound and catchy hooks. She paved the way for the powerhouse that is Adele.

Lady Gaga

Paws up, Little Monsters! Lady Gaga came seemingly from nowhere in the late noughties, bringing the weird and wonderful back into fashion (and leading us to attempt an awful lot of arts and crafts with our hair).

YOU KNOW YOU'RE A CHILD OF THE 2000s WHEN...

You thought *Guitar Hero* would turn you into a superstar guitarist.

The level to which your hopes were raised for your own **"Super Sweet" sixteen** meant you could only have ever been disappointed.

You first became aware of extreme weather with **Hurricane Katrina**.

You wanted to become a **wildlife** cameraperson after seeing *Planet Earth*.

QUIZ

1 What was the "Bieber" haircut?

2 What was the name of Amy Winehouse's famous stacked hairstyle?

3 Long, contrasting extensions were popular in the noughties. What color(s) was Christina Aguilera's hair in the video for "Dirrty"?

4 What style did Halle Berry start sporting in the noughties on her iconic pixie cut?

5 What style of hairclips, commonly used to pin back "hair twists," did every noughties girl wear?

6 Hair color that came in tubes with an applicator was called what?

7 What Elvis-inspired hairstyle topped many a ponytail in the noughties?

8 The ideal noughties highlight was: a) thin or b) chunky?

Answers: 1. Long hair swept to one side; **2.** Beehive; **3.** Black and white; **4.** Spikey pixie; **5.** Butterfly hair clips; **6.** Hair mascara; **7.** The mini quiff; **8.** b) chunky

YOU KNOW YOU'RE A CHILD OF THE 2000s WHEN...

You now unfailingly save all your games thanks to Resetti, the mole from *Animal Crossing*.

When watching **All Grown Up!**
made you realize that just like
Tommy, Dil, Chuckie, and the gang,
you too were getting old.

You've still not recovered
from **Friends** ending.

Your parents still suspect you've
been irrevocably warped by
signals from your mobile phone.

DO YOU REMEMBER...

YouTube
....

YouTube was launched in 2005 and with it went all of our spare time. Let's go way back and remember some golden oldies: *Star Wars* kid, Kelly and her shoes, Auto-Tune the News. And you can't forget that classic Charlie bit my finger! Oh, Charlie, you scamp.

Facebook
....

Remember when you spent hours a day poking people on Facebook and your grandparents didn't even know what it was, let alone had a cute couple's account on it? When you spent time topping up your Facebook aquarium and had to get really creative with how you wrote statuses because of the strange format? Ah, us, too.

BARACK OBAMA

It was 2008 and America had just elected some kind of superhero. Or at least that's the impression that we got, what with all the posters, the rejoicing—oh yes, and the Nobel Peace Prize. No pressure, Barack, no pressure at all.

YOU KNOW YOU'RE
A CHILD OF THE
2000s
WHEN...

You're still collecting the pieces
of your tiny mind after reading
The God Delusion.

You spent the entire decade preparing for the **Digital Switchover**, which you thought would be a teensy bit more dramatic than it eventually was.

You know that when helping a friend move in, you should always remember those wise words from Ross: "**PIVOT, PIVOT!**"

You still think *Slumdog Millionaire* is the greatest love story ever told.

QUIZ

 Sienna Miller was credited with popularising what style of fashion?

 After they moved on from acting, mega-rich twins Mary-Kate and Ashley Oslen created which fashion house?

 What was the name of the jeans with waistlines that were more hipline?

 Celebrities popularized which brand of velour tracksuit?

5 What sleeveless upper-body garment was wildly popular and often worn without a shirt?

 6 What was the optimum length of a cardigan?

 7 What was the name of the brand of comfortable boot that originated in Australia?

8 What hat in the flat-cap family was popular in the noughties?

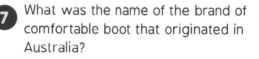

YOU KNOW YOU'RE A CHILD OF THE 2000s WHEN...

You're anxiously waiting for the arthritis you were meant to get from all of the **finger snapping** you did.

You had a sneaky google of "Is it OK to be attracted to blue giants?" after watching **Avatar**.

You sang along to the **Jonas Brothers'** 2007 AMA performance even though you were definitely "too cool" to like them.

You thought you'd be buried in your **Dickies** shorts.

DO YOU REMEMBER...

iPod products

The adverts were cool, the gadgets were even cooler. At first our minds were blown by the fact that we didn't have to carry our CDs everywhere anymore, then suddenly you could shake your iPod to shuffle it, view cover art and even watch films. The future. It was here.

Nintendo DS

Sorry, PlayStation Portable, but we're team *Zelda* and *Phoenix Wright: Ace Attorney* until we die. Represent.

Nintendo Wii / Wii Fit

Finally! A healthy video game that got our parents off our backs about playing too much. Except ... we couldn't get *them* off the console. No fair, Dad, how am I meant to become a tennis pro like this?

Motorola Razr

Sorry, Nokia—the Razr was everything. Though we may have broken the odd one or two by swinging it open too wildly.

Baby-G watch

We would NEVER take our Baby-G off, to the point that the straps would sometimes fall off our wrists through wear, tear and maybe the tiniest bit of mildew.

Webcam

Oh, webcam. So many regrets. So many things filmed that can never be unfilmed. So much blackmail material held by our friends.

YOU KNOW YOU'RE A CHILD OF THE 2000s WHEN...

You firmly have no memory of a time when it was cool to wear **low-rise jeans** with your thong on show. Nope.

You received **endless belts** for Christmas from your dad, who thought he was making a hilarious joke about your jeans-wearing habits.

You devoured *A Series of Unfortunate Events* during your "edgy" phase.

You still cringe about that time you changed your Facebook **relationship status** to "it's complicated."

QUIZ

ONLY A CHILD OF
THE 2000s WILL KNOW...

 1 What was the preferred manner of wearing your shirt collar?

 2 Complete the name of this trucker hat brand: Von _____

 3 What was the nickname for the popular imitation-mohawk hairstyle?

 4 What was the preferred color for trainers?

5 What was the nickname of the small goatee fashionable in the noughties?

6 What was the name of the shell used in the fashionable chokers of the time?

7 This Palestinian chequered scarf was worn by mildly rebellious teens everywhere. What was it called?

8 What athletic fashion line is known by the initials "A" and "F"?

YOU KNOW YOU'RE
A CHILD OF THE
2000s
WHEN...

Dido's **"White Flag"** is your anthem for your favorite relationship "pairing."

You've yet to throw out
your extensive collection of
phone charms.

You spent hours finding the
perfect dramatic-but-subtle song
lyrics for your **MSN name**.

You regret never making it as a
"Myspace celebrity."

Celebrity name abbreviations

LiLo, J-Lo, Xtina; it seems like we really gave up on writing anything out in full during the noughties. And don't get us started on the couple names. RIP TomKat and your sofa-bouncing ways. RIP Bennifer and all your fake tan. Sniff, RIP Brangelina, we thought you were going to make it!

Orlando Bloom

Reluctant pirate, badass elf, possessor of great hair. Orlando was the noughties teen heartthrob. Just call us Mrs. Legolas Turner.

PARIS HILTON

The term "celebrity" became a bit of a looser definition, with the wildly popular reality TV genre coming to the forefront in the 2000s. Over all your Spencers and your Audrinas reigned Paris, our dead-eyed reality princess.

YOU KNOW YOU'RE A CHILD OF THE 2000s WHEN...

This big **eyebrow trend**
is against everything
you've ever stood for.

You're still hoping **Ozzy Osbourne** will adopt you. Or maybe you can adopt him.

You had to change your **email address** from mentalhamster@ awesomemail.com.

If you bump into friends in the street you shout, **"You shall not pass!"**

QUIZ

 Who voiced Dory, the regal tang fish with short-term memory loss in *Finding Nemo*?

 Slumdog Millionaire is structured around the Indian version of what British game show?

 In *Spider-Man*, starring Tobey Maguire, the main villain was known by what pseudonym?

 The eponymous main character of *Borat* is from what country?

5 Teen comedy *Mean Girls* was written by what comedian?

6 What is Napoleon Dynamite's favorite animal?

7 Who curses Sophie in *Howl's Moving Castle*?

8 In what year was the final *The Lord of the Rings* film, *The Return of the King*, released?

YOU KNOW YOU'RE A CHILD OF THE 2000s WHEN...

Wearing your **studded belt** off-center means you're cool.

You found all your **cheat codes** on a piece of paper the other day.

If asked to, you absolutely could write "boobs" on a **calculator**.

You still hold all your parties at **Laser Quest**.

DO YOU REMEMBER...

Bertie Bott's Every Flavor Beans

We had some real questions about these treats when they came out. Would we really have to eat earwax- and vomit-flavored beans? And the answer was … yes.

Cupcakes

No longer were cupcakes the province of every child's party but the new ultra-cool foodstuff. Celebs were seen toting boxes of them around (like they actually ate them) and we found ourselves spending triple the amount of pocket money than usual just to bag these sugary delights.

Fast Food Nation

You were totally freaked out by what you learned when you watched this film, and swore you would never eat a burger again. Unfortunately, your resolution only lasted twenty-four hours.

Energy drinks

If we couldn't have McDonald's, we could at least have Red Bull and Monster. Energy drinks were kind of healthy, right? Right?

Flavored Coke

Lime Coke, Vanilla Coke, Cherry Coke—we went mad for Coke with even more sugar added. And then we went mad afterward, from all that sugar. Happy days spent bouncing off the wall.

No-Carbs/Atkins

It was a little early for diets for us, but Mom sure had some strange-looking dinners for a while. Still, not as strange as that time Beyoncé drank only maple syrup water to lose weight.

YOU KNOW YOU'RE A CHILD OF THE 2000s WHEN...

You have a copy of **Captain Underpants** tucked into the literary classic you're pretending to read.

You may have hospitalized someone just by passing them while wearing a whole can of **Axe** body spray.

You made meticulously planned, ultimately **crap playlists** to burn onto a CD.

You retook your Harry Potter **Sorting Hat** test until you were in the "right" house.

QUIZ

ONLY A CHILD OF THE 2000s WILL KNOW...

 What Emmy-winning director of *Wheel of Fortune* hosted the show throughout the noughties?

 What MTV show was basically just an excuse for us all to look at ridiculously expensive celebrity houses?

 In *The O.C.*, Marissa Cooper passed away in Ryan Atwood's arms; how did she die?

 A young Paris Hilton and Nicole Richie starred in what 2000s reality show?

5 What was the address of *Desperate Housewives* Susan, Lynette, Bree, and Gabrielle?

6 How long would the wives on *Wife Swap* swap families for?

7 Who did Mila Kunis take over the voice-acting role of Meg from in the second season of *Family Guy*?

8 What TV channel did *My Super Sweet 16* air on?

YOU KNOW YOU'RE A CHILD OF THE 2000s WHEN...

You performed for more people than you'd care to admit on your **VJ Starz Video Karaoke Machine**.

You're scarred from all the times
you tripped on the **dangly bits**
on your cargo pants.

You're still not over the
discrepancy between
Hermione's Yule Ball dress
in the book and in the film.

You're secretly grateful that
scarves are a normal
width again.

DO YOU REMEMBER...

Toys "R" Us

There was one reason and one reason only to accept going shopping with your mom. If you suffered through the trauma of CVS and IKEA then you could go to heaven on earth … Toys "R" Us.

Livestrong Wristbands

As the mid-noughties hit, suddenly we all became philanthropists and campaigned for all sorts of charities. Or at least we bought the wristbands. We were so deep.

MSN MESSENGER

Friendships lived and died on MSN. You could go home from school one day best of pals and the next it was all-out war, just through a misinterpreted message or delayed reply on messenger. Such heady days.

YOU KNOW YOU'RE A CHILD OF THE 2000s WHEN...

You have to hold yourself back from giving your work the **WordArt** treatment.

You have a fave
Olsen sibling.

You're not French but you sure do
have a large collection of **berets**.

You still sort of like
The Phantom Menace.

QUIZ

ONLY A CHILD OF THE 2000s WILL KNOW...

 1 SpongeBob SquarePants lived in a pineapple under the sea, but what was his town called?

 2 *Lizzie McGuire* starred which noughties teen celebrity?

 3 No ordinary teenager, Raven Baxter had what—sometimes imperfect—superpower?

 4 What were the names of the Powerpuff Girls?

5 What colors were Cosmo and Wanda's hair in *The Fairly OddParents*?

6 What was the name of Hannah Montana / Miley Stewart's best friend in the Disney TV show?

7 In the sitcom *How I Met Your Mother*, what creature is tattooed on Ted's lower back?

8 What feline feministas were the OG Disney girl squad and had their own theme tune?

Answers: 1. Bikini Bottom; **2.** Hilary Duff; **3.** Seeing the future; **4.** Blossom, Bubbles, and Buttercup; **5.** Green and pink; **6.** Lilly Truscott; **7.** A butterfly; **8.** The Cheetah Girls

YOU KNOW YOU'RE A CHILD OF THE 2000s WHEN...

You serve your best **Blue Steel** any time you look in the mirror.

You practically hosted a welcoming party for **Planters' Cheez Balls** when they relaunched in 2018.

You're still waiting for that **Hogwarts** letter.

You've seen all these **cold-shoulder** trends before.

DO YOU REMEMBER...

John Cena

He may be a big-shot movie star now, but this guy made his name with his weird and wonderful WWE rap creations. Love him or hate him, you probably wouldn't tell him either way to his face. He's deffo still big enough to crush us.

Usain Bolt

Are there any words to describe the feeling of seeing the world's fastest man smash the record for being fast? Add the cheeky little celly at the end and he smashed our hearts too. What a time to be alive.

Roger Federer

If you want to know who won Wimbledon in the 2000s, then the answer is essentially "Federer." He had his breakthrough in 2003 and then he did it again. And again. And didn't stop doing it until 2008, when Nadal thwarted his attempt to beat Björn Borg's record five straight Wimbledon wins.

Williams Sisters

If you want to know who won *everything* in women's tennis, that would be the Williams sisters. In 2002, they occupied the first and second spot in the rankings and by 2009 they ... still occupied the first and second spots in the rankings (with a few ups and downs in-between).

Lewis Hamilton

Sorry, Jenson Button, but it had been a bit of a sad time for UK motorsports until Lewis Hamilton swept the F1 in 2008. He was cool, he was fast and he was record-breaking, and he gave British F1 fans something to be excited about.

YOU KNOW YOU'RE A CHILD OF THE 2000s WHEN...

You remember when there was no **send receipt** on phones and "I'm sorry, I didn't see the message" was a valid excuse.

You had to watch
Everybody Loves Raymond
when you were off sick.

You still hold a moment of silence
for **Marissa Cooper**.

You still "ironically" substitute
goodbye for "**peace
out, my homies**."

If you're interested in finding out more about our books, find us on Facebook at **Summersdale Publishers** and follow us on Twitter at **@Summersdale**.

www.summersdale.com